WHITE PORTALS

WHITE PORTALS

Poems

Jennifer Holley Lux

Press 53
Winston-Salem

Press 53, LLC
PO Box 30314
Winston-Salem, NC 27130

First Edition

A Tom Lombardo Poetry Selection

Cover design by Kevin Morgan Watson

Cover photograph, "Total Solar Eclipse Over Hopkinsville, Kentucky," NASA Image, Public Domain

Author photo by Laura Holley

Library of Congress Control Number
2017964654

Printed on acid-free paper
ISBN 978-1-941209-74-5

For

my mother, Lorraine Pobat Holley (1943 – 1996)

my husband, Thomas Lux (1946 – 2017)

The author thanks the editors of the following publications in which these poems first appeared:

.45 Magazine: "Positano"
Birmingham Poetry Review: "Kazahana" and "Studland Beach"
Broken Bridge Review: "September"
Caduceus: "Fire Ash" and "Sirens"
Connecticut Review: "Sabbatical"
Decameron: "It"
Gyroscope Review: "Hands"
Louisiana Literature: "Nine Lives" and "The Secret"
The Midwest Quarterly: "The Service of Women"
Northeast Magazine: "Diamond Dust"
The Prose Poem: An International Journal: "The Rubbing"
Taj Mahal Review: "The Passing of Light"
Welter: "Noon"

CONTENTS

INTRODUCTION
by Tom Lombardo, Poetry Series Editor

The core of *White Portals* by Jennifer Holley Lux is a pair of elegy-sequences, like binary black holes that have captured each other, spinning and emitting energy witnessed from history measured in light years. In one sequence, she elegizes her husband, the poet Thomas Lux, and in the other, her beloved mother Lorraine Pobat Holley.

The poet has woven her binary pattern in a web strung with memories and musings in coastal locations, worldwide, that braid together like tissue in our bodies: Positano, Studland Beach, New Guinea, California, and Lux's Connecticut home. Each elegiac thread, woven with the skill of a loomer, contributes to a quilt of death, mourning, and consolation. They all fit into a passionate, beautiful collection, Lux's first.

In the poetics of elegy, the movement to consolation signals the beginning of recovery, of moving on. Consolation has been key to elegiac poetics from the Hellenistic pastoral tradition onward. Though consolation nearly disappeared from Modern/Postmodern elegies due to WWI, the Great Influenza of 1918, WWII, the Holocaust, and nuclear weapons, contemporary elegy seems to have restored order.

The move to pursue consolation after the bleak despair of the inconsolable Modern and Postmodern elegists like Wilfred Owen, Robert Lowell, Anne Sexton, or Ruth Stone, drives the contemporary elegies of Douglas Dunn, Donald Hall, Natasha Trethewey, Cathy Smith Bowers, Satyendra Srivastava, Mary Jo Bang, Kathleen Sheeder Bonanno, and Carol Ann Duffy. Jennifer Holley Lux's collection *White Portals* earns my selection as the most significant elegiac collection in more than a decade. She deserves her seat alongside elegists from Theocritus to Duffy.

Lux, like Donald Hall, elegizes her spouse who was a popular poet dying a slow death from cancer. She does not belabor the vivid, ghastly death mask that Hall presents of Jane Kenyon in his 1996 collection *Without*. Here, the deceased is the Sand Man who experiences a sensory moment with his mourner at his point of death. And like Srivastava and Duffy, Lux elegizes her mother, but not with a final drink of water as they have done, but with something much more personal.

Her panties hang
on the basement line,
dried still for months.
…
I sway beneath
… finger
the crotch, kiss it. ("Mistletoe")

That final kiss of her mother foreshadows the final kiss of her husband Thomas Lux as the Sand Man on a beach, which opens the senses between the mourner and deceased at the point of death.

If I kissed sand lips, would you think me

foolish, naïve? My breath,
soft wind across his body. ("Sand Man")

Ambiguity is unresolved. Is there a final kiss? Here, the elegist allows the reader to decide and interpret. In the elegiac tradition of final kisses, these support the trope and expand it. Both are powerful, and unusual.

White Portals' portals are not always open. Sometimes, readers must unlock them. There are many seeming paradoxes wrapped in this collection. The ocean takes away a beloved's ashes, and then the ocean takes away the gem in the mourner's ring. A father first opens up the distant universe to a young child, then later, the mourner's dead mother beckons from deep water: "My mother's face / seducing me to a deeper place" as she swims from the boat with her father ("Sirens"). The mourner's hands perform caring tasks for her dying husband, while the speaker in a persona poem commits random acts of violence to strangers. The mourner takes pills to keep her from flying like a bird. A dying mother asks "Will you please rub my legs?" ("The Rubbing"). A departing lover's words and touch: "When you said farewell, / you tickled me under the chin, / …. A parting, you said, is no impasse." ("Kazahana") A woman tells a secret to her lover, who begins the stepwise spreading of the secret. In a wonderful Baudelairean prose poem, "The Secret," becomes a poem of release, freedom from imprisonment in grief, and thus signals the beginning of recovery for the mourner. It's the final move to consolation after the death, mourning, and memories: the letting go.

WHITE PORTALS

QUESTION AND ANSWER

Do you fear the smoke or the fire?
I fear grass shooting through ash.

Do you fear the howl or the bite?
I fear footprints in the snow.

Do you fear glaciers melting or waters rising?
I fear the sun that watches coolly.

Do you fear forgetting my name or my face?
I fear I will always remember.

Do you fear birthing or holding the child?
I fear him wanting to crawl back inside.

Do you fear white walls or endless night?
I fear the scream that has no end.

Do you fear too little or too much time?
I fear my answer will have no bearing.

Do you fear being first or last to die?
I fear we will go together.

Do you fear my first kiss or my last?
I fear being caught once, forever.

Do you fear the cross in the sky or the voice of God?
I fear the birds moving as one.

Do you fear today or tomorrow?
Yesterday, I told you "tomorrow."

NINE LIVES

They think I kiss
for love.

I take mouths
like red breath
ballooning my
allotted lives.

Not one suspects
enough to shiver.

I kiss a harlot
to slink down
moon-licked streets,

a colonel to bat
enemies back.

Through rising bubbles,
I kiss a diver

then follow a fugitive's
twig-snap steps
to vanish in the woods'
black well.

The child's lips
make me spook
at what's not there.

I kiss a dancer, air
beneath my claws,

an apple picker
for earth to bear
my shadow more than me.

I kiss an old mother
for the cry that pricks
a household's sleep,

and last, a dying man
so I commit
to ear and blood
the unticking
from which I creep.

WHAT THE CROW DEMANDED

That all birdbaths go dry.
That the pleasure of birds besides himself not be tolerated.
That only he be allowed to drink from the king's hand.
That other crows be hobbled.
That he never be thought a jester.
That the sun brighten when his wings imprint its gold.
That being offered corn, he may freely deny it.
That boys drop their stones.
That mothers, hearing his caw, recall children they gave away,
even for a better life;
that fathers stiffen at the thought of cheap wood
bought for their fathers' coffins.
That all read in his eye that someone is more damned.

THE FLOOD

When the river rose high in the night,
it flooded the town, flushing people
from houses into rowboats.

Arms clasped family clocks
and boxes of jewels. Names
were called aloud, followed

by wind-choked replies. A rooftop child
or cat said *Here*. The name
was called again. Ears

strained in the pause. *But some
do go down*, the bubbles said,
like the brother and sister

who found each other at the end,
clutched, tangled damp limbs, clothes,
hair, like spiders

confounded by their web.
After surrender, last breaths,
faces close like before a kiss, they fell

below the banks of the river, where once
the boy shot redbreasts, the girl wept—
where once four feet outran the river.

RUNAWAY'S RETURN

She buries her shoes by the river.
She drops in coins she did not use.
The river feeds on what she forgets.
In rain, beans wither on poles.

No one has picked the rice.
Will anyone answer when she knocks?

Her people sit around the table,
sucking on the cold, hard memory of her.
She insulted the ancestors. This girl

who once cleaned her grandfather's eye,
filled the birdbath from her hands for luck,
pressed her mother's dress with a hot stone.

As she opens the front gate,
she shapes her mouth around the words
she will tell them:
that she could not help,
that she could not change
what happened the day she left:
that a travelling man chanced on the path
where she wet her lips at the stream.

WORLD BOOK

H for Hummingbird.

In the bound volume,
  Mother's fingers find
    three glossy hatchlings

  cradled in a scientist's
white-gloved palm, their
  needle-nose beaks

    mid-cheep. Someday,
  they'll be quick
among quince trees:

    fan-blade wings at work,
      greener than willows
    at the height of spring,

more vaporous than clouds.
  If with a snapped sprig
    of honeysuckle,

  I lure one plaything
through a jam jar's hole,
  I'll feel wings panic

    against the glass wall—
  unlike the boozy taps
of fireflies' discontent.

  I will crack the lid,
    memorize polished
onyx eyes, emerald

crown, before I tip
  the jar, let jewels
    drain to a sapphire sky.

THE CALLING

After *Adrift* by Steven Callahan

Shipwrecked, unknown days
adrift. You feed a rubber raft
breath through sinking nights,
bone-blinding days.

Boils, blisters, mirage, and dream.
Your gut devours ulcers, purges
bile, sharpens its knife again.

Your tongue flicks bloodied
lips, crusted with salt.
Licking causes hot coals
to roll through your throat.
Only voice left now fire.

Night storms rock you
like a deranged nurse.
In the raft's dark cradle,
you take the rain's beating
but drink your fill,
moaning like a deaf child.

One dawn, your body nearly
pulped by punching waves,
what causes a fish
to jump in your raft?

You rouse, pin
the dorado down,
stab a rusty blade deep.
You cut morsels, savor flesh,
kissing and eating, eating and kissing
the fins, the tail, that shot
the fish, bull's-eye, to you.

Left with entrails, you slice the stomach,
lift from the sac a *second* fish,
heavy, whole, swallowed
moments before the first fish leapt.

A fluke? A gift within a gift? Enough
to make you believe something
wants you to live
to tell this tale
to another soul—
hungry, dying,
but not yet lost at sea.

SEPTEMBER

You saw the blue sky today,
as I did when I awoke and pulled the curtain aside.
Yes, I was happy.
I pressed my palm to the window;
it was cold, so I pulled away.

It was windy, and the leaves on the very tops of the trees
were yellow and red.

Yes, I took a walk and passed a cemetery.
I thought of death,
as I think you have, too.

I imagined I was a heroine in a favorite novel:
enlightened, morbid, friendless.
But you know friends are unnecessary
and only a burden on days like today.

Yes, I came home when my fingertips and ears became numb
and my imagination tired.

I wished it were November, so I could build a fire,
hot and spitting.
It is foolishly early for one now.
So I put on my father's cardigan
with sleeves that fall past my knuckles.
Yes, I was warm enough.
I ate soup for lunch, pretending I was young,
but knowing I was old,
as you might have expected.

HANDS

I will wash my hands. With water, with soap. I will wash with vigor. And often. Today, I touched machines inside and out. Their greased gears. Their levers handled by a thousand men. Before I touch myself again, I will pluck petals of soiled clothes. I will kill germs before they sink unseen through skin. I will make myself worthy of touch. I will wash my hands of yesterday's fights and ready them for today's. As I exit the shower, I view in the mirror how red hands dangle from long, white arms. Like a stranger's hands sewn on my wrists. Too much red enlarges my hands. I cannot control what they will do. As in late last night. I entered a donut shop to wash my hands. A lady stood in my way. She would not let me through the line. My hands, they hit her. I said "I'm sorry," but no one heard because everyone was yelling and the lights were bright. They surprised me by pointing at my chest instead of my hands. They cannot see what I have done right. The nights I listened for morning birds, letting a woman beside me sleep. Not touching her at all. Sometimes my hands storm. I am blamed for this. If people saw how I hold back. If they saw the bruises I have not let happen because I hold back, they would love me. At every step, my hands, like wings on a bird. You see? My hands, they fly.

RATTLE

When you decided
to go to sleep,
to let them open
your legs and suck
me out, I

let the body
go, but burrowed
my spirit deep in your flesh
against the pull,
a fast storm
that left nothing
the same.

They looked in
with lit scopes
but could not see me.
They kneaded your stomach
yet could not feel me.

I rode your blood
upstream to find
its beating source.
There I clung
to a flapping valve.
When you woke
I rattled it wildly.

You pressed
your hand to your chest,
sensing a murmur,
sensing your heart trying
to tell you
something.

UNBORN

A schoolroom perfumed
like a pond overlaid with leaves
displays splayed monarchs,
tinkling test tubes,
stern microscopes,
jars with mud, sludge,
jars with tan reeds
bent like fingers.

A creature, bruise-yellow,
glows in pink ooze.
Its body curves into itself
to fit the jar, nearly outgrown.
Its mouth, pinched.
A twitch?

It could be a human fetus,
but my little sister was never so small.
Do orange ears mean it's a kitten?

I press the lukewarm lid.
A pulse.
Fluorescent lights flicker and fizz.

It'll come out fine
by the end of the year:
a dripping, life-stunned baby
lifted by the teacher's hands
to the *oohs* of circling children.

DIRT EATERS

Don't talk to those who eat the dirt.
Those children squat in shady skirts
around the farm's un-mooing barns,
around tool sheds, coffin-closed.

Don't talk to them, we hear, we're told.
Play inside with things we've not
yet sold. A broom can be your groom.
A balled-up shirt, just so, a baby.

Don't talk to children who claw earth
and seize chunks, moist chocolate
brown beneath a sun-baked crust.
Cave-cold, close to the sweat-dripped

upper lip, before first nibble,
dirt tickles hairs around the mouth.
It smells of worms and ferns. Breathe in.
It smells of roots to make us grow.

ALL THE ALMOSTS

When cabinets under sinks
weren't locked to keep
our tiny paws out
of the small city
of poisons glowing
lemon, lime, and blue.

That we rode
bikes, hands high
in unsteady surrender,
as handlebars wobbled
and cars screeched
around the curve,
then upon us,
swerved.

That we didn't play
with matches too much
in the attic of the barn
on bales of hay.

That blister-greased palms
never slipped from branches
when shrieking kids
heckled us higher.

That window screens
that we leaned into
held each cast
of forehead and hands.

That the stranger in the park
lured a child
whose abandoned swing,
still swinging, we raced to,
reaching for the still-warm chain.

That we pumped legs harder,
enlarging the arc
of wild abandon,
never knowing our luck.

SAND MAN

I have seen them—on long stretches
of glowing golden sand in Miami,
Dubai, Anguilla—reclining
sand men and sand women,
smoothed over, patted by sand

sculptors, until their limbs grow taut,
the garnet inside their eyes winks noon.
It was like that, like those recumbent
figures, like a mermaid or Triton,
but with him, no rippled sand hair

curled around a waist, no crown
topped a wild, wave-swept mane,
no fishtail forked up from the beach.
His flank so smooth, you would have thought
him real. His skin glowed quartz. Some

redder stones freckled the abdomen.
Where his sculptor drizzled water,
blue rivers darkened calves and hands.
The stillness of his open eyes—
like the blank globes on a sand man's face.

I've heard of women who fall
in love with marble statues and wish
to ease open cold lips with a
passionate tongue. It was like that, too.
I wrote with my fingers my desire,

tracing the dip below his ribs—
a valley in which I could fall and fall.
My head upon his chest, I viewed
his scooped-out cheek, his whittled jaw.
His hands crossed on his chest, no sign

of warrior. Nothing of sage, senator,
or poet. Nothing in it but
a man of sand, a sand man
whose fingers were slender batons.
If I kissed sand lips, would you think me

foolish, naïve? My breath,
soft wind across his body.
We are not troubled by great winds here.
He did not fly away but washed
back to the place from which he was born.

FIRE ASH

Tonight, I swim in you
off the beach where I
released your ashes to gusts
of westerly wind, to waves'
whitecaps, to deep cracks
in mica-speckled stones.
As for fire, you were fire
birthed in my palm's cup.
How did I ever learn
to hold it, yet feel no burn?

Tonight, I wade in stars'
reflections that itch
like minnows' glitter-backs.
You return high above me
like a pocketful of coins
tossed to the deep of the sky.
You wreathe my bobbing head
with underwater flames.

LULLAY

Waking and sleeping,
dreaming and waking,
were the same to you:
a tumbling in your mother's
viscous dark.

Is heaven another
expanding space
through which you swim
toward a prick of light—
a distant, dying sun?

SABBATICAL

Here in this desert's only house, our dome,
at night, my father sits me down before
a giant telescope, and says, *Look in that glass.*
Peering into a dime-sized hole, I can't

see anything. I hear him step around
the great machine. *Look now.* He flips
a hidden switch; a black cloth falls away
suddenly to show the universe fixing

to get a better look at me. I hold
my breath, poised not to startle the galaxy.
Skittish, the sky kicks a dust cloud of stars falling
although they disappear before they land.

I hope you like it here, my father says.
We'll be staying a year, you know.
Last week, he signed me out of school where all
the boys ran faster, hit balls farther,

and jumped higher than I did. But now I live
inside a castle where sky bows down to me.
Back home, the boys chase one another around
the old baseball diamond behind the gym,

day after day. They'll never see I'm gone.

PILLS

I take a pill in the morning, so I live to thank the end of the day. A pill to keep my head beneath the dark cloud, to keep me low. I take a pill to carry me up through the clouds, where no one sees the sun but me. I take pills that provide every vitamin I need. I take a pill to make my stomach feel full. Each day, from a little, pink box, I take a pill that keeps me from having babies. When I forget to take it, I take another pill that makes me vomit, but stops the baby. It makes me bleed sooner and longer, and gives me cramps for which I take a pill. If the pill to stop the baby doesn't work, I take another pill to get rid of the baby, then four more pills to make sure it's gone for real. Doctors give me pills to make me forget I did this. If I start to weep on the street, I take a pill because the earth is about to crack open between my legs. I take pills to sleep, pills to wake up, pills to make me recall what I need to do each day, where to go, my name. I take pills to keep me from howling at the moon. From prowling with the cats at night. I take pills that turn up the corners of my mouth when I meet people. That restrain me from climbing to the roof and unfolding my wings. From flying off like a bird, the last of its kind.

THE SERVICE OF WOMEN

New Guinea, 1944

As a WAC, I cleaned men's teeth,
replaced rot with gold.
I did not dance or sing with women
on the South Pacific beach.
Our genius lay in outsmarting rats.

I cut my feet on coconut shells
that littered the sands of Oro Bay.
I pulled the rope on the mission bell
to call children to school.
The hills called back, drumming.

Native children learned our ways.
Our men were shot by Japanese.
Palms tilted towards the bay.
Our barracks had no windows.
Our barracks did not tilt towards the sea.

Lore claimed spirits lived in rocks.
If moved, they would return.
Natives crept, wearing masks
with humans' hair and pigs' teeth.
Girls grinned over ebony bowls

overfilled with bukabuk and golden apples,
given as gifts to our hungry men.
Parrots alighted from mangrove trees
like leaves shook free by a sudden storm,
wings thundering.

At every chance, men surrounded our camp.
They pushed their fingers through the fence,
offering rings handmade from coins.
Their faces looked like masks with pigs' teeth.
Their hair looked so real.

Some women blushed, accepting trinkets.
I was not girlish.
One day, I threw a rock in the bay
out of spite, and felt joyful.
Its weight would not be felt again.

That night, in my bunk, a hand cupped my mouth.
A body fell on me like earth,
pressing me back to my seedling start.
I became like nothing until
a stone rose in my throat.

When did he leave? I do not know.
Moonlight shone through cracks
of the barracks' walls.
I stood up shaking and went to pee.
Seed fell in the latrine.

Women later bathed in pairs,
pulled beds closer.
Six men were hanged.
The birds returned to the trees.
The men backed off the fence.

I showed the doctor where to feel
the rock that never came to term.
He never touched me deep enough.
I returned home to Rochester, New York.
I was never meant to be a bride.

NOCTURNE

Hot and awake in downtown HoJo,
I turn on the light, grab Visine,
and feel for lumps I've come to know.
The backyard road scrapes Chicago,
a grid work of steel and routine
where to school I'm about to go
unless my future's bred in the bone.
Curled up tight like an embryo,
into my knees I sing
arias to make dark thoughts go.
Night watches like a one-eyed crow,
face turned from a deathbed scene.
If it goes blind on me, I'll know
to pack my things and go.

THE PASSING OF LIGHT

Whenever you walk by the fountain
that gushes, foams, and forms light-drops,
fall down on your knees on the damp grass,
let mist descend on your body.

Your coat of invisible water,
mosaic of fragments of mirrors,
refracts your flat world into rainbows.

You are not light, but the passing
of light, like a fish with gold scales
that hints at sea-surface an instant
and sears like the eye of God flashing,

then stabs as it leaves you forever—
consumed by the waves of the ocean.

GENESIS

Novocain numbed the girl's gums with a prick.
Tools scraped enamel, whizzed and drilled
over the water-pik's squirt, the air-tube's suck.

The man whose hands loomed over her head
offered her a job. She told him *yes* with a silver smile.
The spittoon gurgled behind. She grew intimate with

the popped abscess, the impacted tooth extraction,
the cracked incisor, and loved most of all
the x-ray process: film jammed

between cheek and molars, the low-light room,
flick of a switch, a zap, skeleton
grins buried in drawers. My theory is

her cancer began to develop then
despite lead aprons. The dentist liked her
reliability. They parted at night on the stoop.

In shop windows, she watched her milky figure
emerge and retreat, imagined a boy at her side.
Under her coat wrapped against the wind,

buds mutated as she dreamed.

UNVEILING

Do you want to see?
my mother asks,
tugging her nightgown
with just one hill
on a chest of primroses.

I've come home
from a year haunting
museums. Always
female nudes
always missing
a toe, an arm,
or breast.
Always a cold
hall, hushing.

I've come home
to a modern sculpture
who peppers an egg
for late breakfast
by a sun-tossed sea.

She lifts an eyebrow.
Sure, I say.

Olive fingers
loosen buttons,
unveiling a plain
of buckled skin
stapled shut.

She lowers her gaze.

The mockingbird sings stolen reveries.
Tomatoes ripen on the sill.
Lace curtains breathe in the wind.
Sunlight pulses on her wrists.
All things move and grow around her—

around, and still within.

THE RUBBING

We both wake up in the night. On her way from the bathroom, she meets me in the kitchen, a glass of water in my hand. *Will you please rub my legs?* she asks. I take her arm, walk her back to bed. She stretches on top of the quilt, rolls on her stomach, tugs off her turban, and runs her fingers through her scalp's gray fuzz. I lean over to stroke it, too, before dousing my hands in rubbing alcohol. I massage her calves until my hands burn from the heat between us. *All over,* she says. I rise up the backs of her knees. Then up her thighs. She moans as if the pain sharpens under my care. I notice the open door and wish I had shut it. I find the creases higher on her legs and slide the sides of my palms in them, brushing along the lace hem of her nightgown. *Do you hurt all over?* I ask. *Yes,* she says, *even higher.* She quiets as I lift her gown and let it pool in the small of her back. She wears nothing else. I take her buttocks in my hands, knead them. I now know how soft and slack my own skin will feel in thirty years. We make no sound to travel through walls, to wake my sister so she creeps in to see. Our mother, on her stomach, her gown hitched to her waist. Me, straddled over her body, about to collapse, on my knees.

POSITANO

The books say sirens throated opiate wind
from rocks along the Positano coast.
Sailors sick of sailors heard an end
to sugarless nights, envisioned red-haired hosts

whose bodies welcomed men like soft dunes,
whose tongues unglued salt from calloused skin
and never twisted words to trap a groom.
I've traveled here for something to begin.

The coughing bus ascends the cliff. Down,
spinning seas surround fateful rocks
where no one sits and sings, where white foam
clings like old men's beards. Above, a flock

of seagulls wrenches from their briny souls
a wind-sucked song. The busman brakes, and rolls.

ON LOOKING THROUGH MY FIRST EYEGLASSES

I reached and missed my purse on the table.
What distant feet I had!
My mother seemed so far.
As she paid the bill, I saw her clearly,
as if I'd never seen her before.
I held her arm to keep myself stable.

We pushed open the office door,
walked into the sun—what sun!
Each object broke from its gauzy shell.
Each leaf, each twig, each blade of grass
sharpened its beckoning tip.
A school bus raced along the street—a comet
flashing on earth. Space came to me!

A god with first creation, I longed to stroke
each thin petal upon one dandelion.
I wanted to float home,
but Mom brought the station wagon.
So we drove down that long, black road,
as if in a boat on long, black river
throwing back the light of the stars.
And I, who knew so little,
could name each one.

UNDER STARS

Out of the car, my mother clutched my wrist
so fiercely I feared kissing her.
She stared at the sky. The Big Dipper
tipped its curl of stars that night
for her to sip from its ladle.

We shuffled up porch stairs,
past flowerpots that spun from hooks,
lost petals to the wind.
Back in the car, my father fumbled
in her bags for medication.

She said, *I've smelled salt air*
since Portland Bridge and breathed
it deep inside. Everything
can be cured by the sea. I listened
hard. The ebb tide held.

We had one month left of summer.
We leaned forward, linked together.
Though she folded like a doll in my arms,
I had no doubt she would recover.

SIRENS

We sailed alone as always, Dad and I.
He held the wheel and left me free to stake
the windswept bow, my gaze fixed on the sky.
He kept one eye ahead, one on our wake.

When sun drowned us mid-afternoon, the wind
died. Our pregnant sails fell.
I stripped to my suit and jumped to give the fish
my flesh, emerged out of my shell.

My dad descended, too. We swam around
the boat, until, worn out, he climbed on deck.
Still not done, I dove until I found
fingers on my neck,

and below the waves, my mother's face
seducing me to a deeper place.

MISTLETOE

Her panties hang
on the basement line,
dried stiff for months.
My hands drip
from washing clothes.
I hear upstairs
the piano pound
"What Child Is This?"
I sway beneath
the panties, finger
the crotch, kiss it.

AFTER THE APPLE, EVE

Scare bees away. They obey. Lick honey straight from the comb. It's a hot day. Run off to where it's hotter. Suck on sugarcane, then dance to shake the high out of your bones. You're on a roll now. Sneak into your neighbor's garden. Steal the biggest melon and run off into the woods. Feel its weight in your arms. Feel it bump against your stomach. Run until you reach a clearing. Split the melon over a rock. Look in the grass for the deep-red heart kept cool all summer long. Eat it. Spit seeds as far as you're able. Not far away, a cow grazes. Walk up and squat beneath the taut belly. Pull a teat to fill the cup of your mouth. Guzzle it warm. Yes. This is your neighbor's cow. You're in for it now. Climb a peach tree until you reach the highest fruit. The more scratches, the better. Snap off a peach and pierce its fur with your teeth. Suck juice before it drips. Come down, still not full. Pull rutabagas from the earth. Feel roots pulling back. Let yourself win. Run. Run on rivers. Just to be fast. Run where you want, away from where you came. Stop. Look around this new forest. Fall on your knees. Pick berries that have no names. Swallow them whole.

KAZAHANA

That winter in Japan,
you draped a fur coat
over my shoulders
when I turned away
to examine a butterfly
in a hothouse.

*

In the streets, no one
ever talked to me.
The streets, to me, were paved
with people.
If I were a carriage, I would roll
over them.

*

But *you* spoke two languages,
maybe more? You wrapped me
tight in your down comforter
like a swaddled baby, and I
wiggled, laughed, even though
I could not move—was caught.

*

When Siberian winds howled
like a ghost army of warlords racing
down the mountain,
lashing people's faces red
with icy whips,
I lay in your side,
one of your ribs.

*

When you said farewell,
you tickled me under the chin,
saying you'd be home
before I'd realize you were gone.

*

A parting, you said, is no impasse,
no more
than frozen ground is an impasse
to spring. What is meant
to be will come to pass.

*

Snowflakes smashed at the window.
Kazahana, you told me,
the word meaning "wind-flowers."
If I caught one on my tongue,
and it took root,
a garden of cold words would grow.

NOON

Even the time
you waited for me
    with an outstretched

        blue towel
    as I stumbled out
        of the breaking waves,

    I felt I was falling.

        Maybe it was
    the invisible gulls

        screeching in the folds
    of the clear sky
        that made me dizzy,

or sails dripping
    off the horizon.

You held my head
        fast to your chest

    as surf thundered
and water licked
            our ankles with foam.

    Above the din,

two high-pitched voices
    called us to return,

        separately, home.

YELLOW DRAGON

Throughout our region, orange trees'
leaves grow maps of jaundiced rivers
running through verdant lands.

Disease of yellow dragon, or *huanglongbing*,
as Chinese call it,
sours our only crop,
our fleshy, sweet-tang fruits.

No oranges hang here now, only
green-tinged tumors.
Their skin, peeled back,
exposes pith—
fibrous white webs.

If you detach a segment,
pierce thumbnails through membrane,
tear it in two,
no juice drips down your wrists.
Under membrane: palsied pulp.

Don't eat this fruit.
Placed on the tongue, the fruit imparts
a bitter truth our elders knew,
unwanted after known,
and never, after, unknown…

You may ask, "What happened
to all who toiled here,
who tended the trees,
who picked the fruits,
who wove the baskets
into which fruits fell
from honeyed hands?"

Scientists told us:
"Move to the mountains."
The transmitter of disease,
they said, the citrus psyllid, sap-sucking
plant louse, cannot fly
to high altitudes to which we
can train our lungs to breathe.

In our absence, from the mountain peak,
we study our distant trees on which
the psyllid swarm's patina
falls like an ancient veil.

IT

She doesn't believe it. Then she does because friends do. A girl in class loses it on a desk after school. At a party, she plays spin the bottle. The bottle stops on her, and a boy punches the air. She picks the queen from a deck of cards: twelve minutes, house rules. Her friends lock her in the bathroom. She doesn't know when to swallow. She gets a boyfriend who gives her a gold chain. Two of her friends have done it. She and her boyfriend talk children. They can't agree on the point of religion, so they break up. She dates a man who lies by her side fully dressed. Then one who requests that she strip to "Foxy Lady." Another tries to pry her open with his finger and his tongue. But no. She begins to dress in the Virgin's radiant blue. Then in paler, paler blues she dresses. She turns at last to white. At night she prays, "I'm ready if you'll have me." He comes to her in voices. In winter, she buys a white parka with a fur hood. One afternoon, she walks to the store for milk down streets walled with plowed snow from a week of storms. It begins to fall again. It lands on her lashes and stays. "Yes," she says, "as it should be." No longer pavement beneath her boots. "Yes, yes." She lifts her face, if a face it be. Snow covers her, flake by flake, until she's gone.

HE MAKETH ME

He maketh me to lie down
on the Isle of Shoals, on a flat rock
mat glinting garnet and granite
in the cold spring haze.
He maketh me to call this isle bedfellow.

A ship transported me here one night,
and the captain's order (as a graphite cloud
sketched out the moon) compelled me
to disembark. There was no kindness
or unkindness in the captain.
His voice moved me like the end of a blunt stick.
He did as he was told.

The first fog-draped morning, I understood
my work, though I know not how:
to measure wingspans of hatchling terns.
I record in a book how fewer and fewer
fish in the sea make for
littler and littler slap-unhappy food
the terns plunge-pluck

to feed their young. Both parents feed them,
but still not enough. How do I know?
Something metallic in the hatchling cries,
from the guts of those who feed them, too.

He maketh me, in storms, retreat to the lighthouse,
the abandoned column on a rock-strewn hill.
I go inside but crouch by the door.
I stay only if I see a swift way out
for the lighthouse smells of rain-quenched burns.

Do birds become my friends?
Their screech-dives toward my head increase.
I pad the inside of my hat with rags.
To terns, I am akin to gulls: a predator
who puts her scent
on every buff-brown speckled egg,
on every hatchling's wing.

He maketh me to mark
the fury of terns in flight:
sloped black heads, frosted breasts,
smoky wings and tails—
newspapers undone by wind.

STUDLAND BEACH

After a painting by Vanessa Bell

A tent stands on the sand,
at the very edge of sand,
a white portal to the sea,
a well-lit door to the sea,
on cobalt, a cube of sugar.

The sea is flat as a wall,
and the sand hard as stone.
The tent waves a white flag.
Inside, clothes come off.
Inside, one swims in light.

A woman may go inside,
a woman erect as a column,
her back to all her children.
No breeze billows her skirt.
She knows what is inside.

She may, however, lift
the flap to the white womb
where soft sun loiters
and children's voices are far,
heard through pillows.

If she goes inside,
she might never return.
She might undress and stay
until the children's voices
die out like the light.

She might not come out
the next summer, or the next.
No one will mention the fact.
The children will go on.
No need for goodbye.

DIAMOND DUST

Beneath the hurricane's wide-open eye,
beneath the moon that steps across the sky
like an angel afraid to fall, we strip
in ones and twos along the wall that keeps
our houses safe against the sea.

We pull down jeans, unbutton shirts, unhook
bras, and rub our hands in between the stones
to find deep gaps in which to hide our soft
shed skins. Walking apart to conceal our grins,
we stumble on rocks into the sea.

Spirits conjured sheer-white into this world,
together we find what parts of us light loves—
the milky undersides of arms and wrists;
on Jessica, the periwinkle twists
upon her breasts; on Michael's hips,

the curves on which he cups his hands. Light strokes
the hair Linda secures behind her ear,
and Jennifer's lips, glittering black, unclasped
to let a scream slide out, as she's the first
to vanish underwater, to come

up painted silver-blue. We all dive in
to be as beautiful as she, to shine scuffed parts
which in the day we wish away.
Only storm waves keep us from swimming out
and catching hold of night's tail.

ELEPHANT SEALS

They looked like logs until they howled.
On the California coast below
a guard-railed cliff, on the sun-bleached
morning beach, elephant seals

covered bodies with sand, flapping
flippers to coat round bellies,
seasoning themselves for a giant's feast.
When one growled, I shuddered, glad

to be high on land, my car still running
not far behind. They brushed and rolled,
dead skin peeling off in scrolls,
patches washing away with the tide.

When one cried out, I cringed for its pain.
But what did I know of the seal's tongue
or what skin felt like during yearly molting?
Others parked, circled to watch.

Don't get close, you said.
But how could they hurt us—
no legs, no arms? How could flippers
not much larger than my feet

mobilize bodies big as barrels
to lurch forward, bite off my face?
But those teeth—! I held back,
snorts and whiskery old-man jowls

cursing rudely, burping thunder.
These living boulders had rolled straight
out of the great Pacific. At sea
they had slurped rays, ratfish, squid.

Now digested. They groaned for more.
These bellies, the ocean's empty graves,
dark, risen, and speaking loudly—
here, among us, in California!

SUDDEN GRAVITY

As I strolled ankle-deep along the sea,
when did the diamond in my ring
slip from its prongs and sink?
I shielded my eyes to better see
how sand's stretched arms gleamed.
I backwards read the shore to my beginning
to find Earth had snatched back her thing
with a fist of sudden gravity.

But I, too, want back what I possessed
and lost—a ghost tethered to my soul—
and grow obsessed
in finding the piece that made me whole.
But I, unlike Earth, cannot pull home
the life I carried, lighter than a stone.

THE CATCH

All I needed was a long net
with one end free at low tide.
A boy came running,

grabbed an end. We got to work.
Our toes hooked in squelching sand.
We dragged hard.

A horseshoe crab, like a dead soldier's
helmeted head, roved the pewter shore.
We shooed black flies, slapped mosquitoes,
gave wide berth to wound-red jellies,
pulled a load toward land.

Kids circled around to help peel back
folds of rope. Crabs clawed out.
In our clutches: seaweed, crawfish,
flicking gobs of minnows
that tail-tickled our hovering hands.

Sure we could find treasure
with a deeper drag, farther out,
we carried the net back to water,
submerged and shimmied it,
let captives go.

Moving dumbly at first,
minnows floated limply.
Then they sobered, snapped to it
like the Health-Ed film
of fat-headed sperm
doggedly wagging tails.

All around us, minnow on minnow,
a gold, gelatinous sea.
I stood among them,
feeling nothing.

THE SECRET

A woman who lost a husband decides to tell his secret to her lover in bed. He takes the secret home in his heart and whispers it into his wife's ear while she sleeps. The next day, she says such strange things to her children, things she has never said before, things she surely does not mean. One of these things is the secret. Two of the children pay her no mind, but one child does, and he carries the secret with him to school. He tells the secret to his friend. This friend speaks little. So he imparts the secret to his dog, the only creature in the world who understands him. The secret weighs heavily on the dog's mind. When set free in the yard, he barks the secret. Everyone in the neighborhood is trying to sleep, so they ignore the secret. In the dry, hot summer night, the secret blows into the barking dust. Wind trumpets the secret up, up, up! It carries the secret across town, where a woman in bed parts her lips. She inhales the secret, and the secret enters her dreams. All night, her eyelashes flutter as if a heavy breeze breathes continuously over her body. When first light knocks and her eyelids lift, a curtain falls. She rarely remembers dreams. But years later, walking one day in the city, hit by a sudden gust of wind, she remembers the secret.

ACKNOWLEDGMENTS

The writing of this book was supported by grants from Aetna and the University of Connecticut. I thank my family, friends, and teachers for their encouragement, and Tom Lombardo for his editorial advice in the final stages of this book.

Jennifer Holley Lux

Jennifer Holley Lux's poems have appeared in *Birmingham Poetry Review, Connecticut Review, The Midwest Quarterly* and *The Prose Poem: An International Journal.* She has lived most of her life in Connecticut but currently resides in Atlanta. She works at the Georgia Institute of Technology.

www.ingramcontent.com/pod-product-compliance
Lightning Source LLC
LaVergne TN
LVHW041346080426

835512LV00006B/645